GALATIANS, TITUS, & PHILEMON

FREEDOM IN CHRIST

13 Studies for Individuals or Groups

WHITNEY   KUNIHOLM

Harold Shaw Publishers • Wheaton, Illinois

CONTENTS

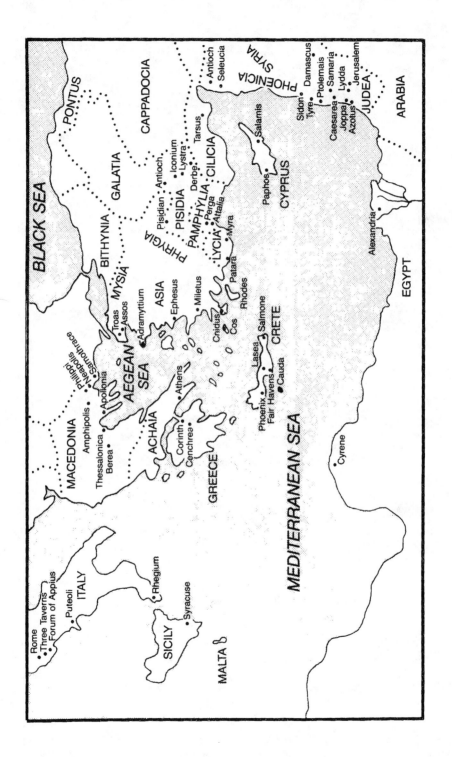

HOW TO USE THIS STUDYGUIDE

Fisherman studyguides are based on the inductive approach to Bible study. Inductive study is discovery study; we discover what the Bible says as we ask questions about its content and search for answers. This is quite different from the process in which a teacher *tells* a group *about* the Bible and what it means and what to do about it. In inductive study God speaks directly to each of us through his Word.

A group functions best when a leader keeps the discussion on target, but this leader is neither the teacher nor the "answer person." A leader's responsibility is to *ask*—not *tell*. The answers come from the text itself as group members examine, discuss, and think together about the passage.

There are four kinds of questions in each study. The first is an *approach question*. Used before the Bible passage is read, this question breaks the ice and helps you focus on the topic of the Bible study. It begins to reveal where thoughts and feelings need to be transformed by Scripture.

Some of the earlier questions in each study are *observation questions* designed to help you find out basic facts—who, what, where, when, and how.

When you know what the Bible says you need to ask, *What does it mean?* These *interpretation questions* help you to discover the writer's basic message.

Application questions ask, *What does it mean to me?* They challenge you to live out the Scripture's life-transforming message.

Fisherman studyguides provide spaces between questions for jotting down responses and related questions you would like to raise in the group. Each group member should have a copy of the studyguide and may take a turn in leading the group.

For consistency, Fisherman guides are written from the *New International Version*. But a group should feel free to use the NIV or any other accurate, modern translation of the Bible such as the *New Living Translation*, the *New Revised Standard Version*, the *New Jerusalem Bible*, or the *Good News Bible*. (Other paraphrases of the Bible may be referred to when additional help is needed.) Bible commentaries should not be brought to a Bible study because they tend to dampen discussion and keep people from thinking for themselves.

SUGGESTIONS FOR GROUP LEADERS

1. Read and study the Bible passage thoroughly beforehand, grasping its themes and applying its teachings for yourself. Pray that the Holy Spirit will "guide you into truth" so that your leadership will guide others.

2. If the studyguide's questions ever seem ambiguous or unnatural to you, rephrase them, feeling free to add others that seem necessary to bring out the meaning of a verse.

3. Begin (and end) the study promptly. Start by asking someone to pray for God's help. Remember, the Holy Spirit is the teacher, not you!

4. Ask for volunteers to read the passages out loud.

5. As you ask the studyguide's questions in sequence, encourage everyone to participate in the discussion. If some are silent, ask, "What do you think, Heather?" or, "Dan, what can you add to that answer?" or suggest, "Let's have an answer from someone who hasn't spoken up yet."

6. If a question comes up that you can't answer, don't be afraid to admit that you're baffled! Assign the topic as a research project for someone to report on next week.

7. Keep the discussion moving and focused. Though tangents will inevitably be introduced, you can bring the discussion back to the topic at hand. Learn to pace the discussion so that you finish a study each session you meet.

8. Don't be afraid of silences: some questions take time to answer and some people need time to gather courage to speak. If silence persists, rephrase your question, but resist the temptation to answer it yourself.

9. If someone comes up with an answer that is clearly illogical or unbiblical, ask him or her for further clarification: "What verse suggests that to you?"

10. Discourage Bible-hopping and overuse of cross-references. Learn all you can from *this* passage, along with a few important references suggested in the studyguide.

11. Some questions are marked with a ♦. This indicates that further information is available in the Leader's Notes at the back of the guide.

12. For further information on getting a new Bible study group started and keeping it functioning effectively, read Gladys Hunt's *You Can Start a Bible Study Group* and *Pilgrims in Progress: Growing through Groups* by Jim and Carol Plueddemann.

SUGGESTIONS FOR GROUP MEMBERS

1. Learn and apply the following ground rules for effective Bible study. (If new members join the group later, review these guidelines with the whole group.)

2. Remember that your goal is to learn all that you can *from the Bible passage being studied.* Let it speak for itself without using Bible commentaries or other Bible passages. There is more than enough in each assigned passage to keep your group productively occupied for one session. Sticking to the passage saves the group from insecurity and confusion.

3. Avoid the temptation to bring up those fascinating tangents that don't really grow out of the passage you are discussing. If the topic is of common interest, you can bring it up later in informal conversation following the study. Meanwhile, help each other stick to the subject!

4. Encourage each other to participate. People remember best what they discover and verbalize for themselves. Some people are naturally shyer than others, or they may be afraid of making a mistake. If your discussion is free and friendly and you show real interest in what other group members think and feel, they will be more likely to speak up. Remember, the more people involved in a discussion, the richer it will be.

5. Guard yourself from answering too many questions or talking too much. Give others a chance to express themselves. If you are one who participates easily, discipline yourself by counting to ten before you open your mouth!

6. Make personal, honest applications and commit yourself to letting God's Word change you.

INTRODUCTION TO GALATIANS

Galatians is a passionate letter written to defend the essence of the Good News. Salvation is by faith alone! And God's family equally embraces Jew and Gentile, male and female, slave and free.

Jews and Gentiles had always been separate and contemptuous of each other. But in Christ they were suddenly united and equal recipients of God's blessing. However, some Jewish Christians were trying to impose the old Mosaic Law (specifically circumcision) on the Gentile believers as a prerequisite for salvation. So when Paul returned to Antioch after completing his first missionary journey around A.D. 49, he dashed off a strong letter to defend the gospel message he had preached in Galatia.

In Galatians we sense the power of the apostle Paul's personality. He was sometimes angry, at other times exasperated; sometimes humble, yet often incredibly bold. But all the time he was committed to one goal: convincing his readers that the way to God is not through some combination of Christianity and Judaism or Christianity plus anything else, but rather through faith in Christ alone. This is the Good News!

SENT BY GOD

Galatians 1:1-10

The apostle Paul usually began his letters with a warm greeting followed by words of praise and encouragement—but not this letter! Here he "comes out swinging." To put it bluntly, he is boiling mad.

One way the false teachers were attempting to gain credibility was by attacking Paul's personal credentials. They said Paul wasn't really an apostle, since he wasn't one of the original Twelve. They insinuated that he had no authority to preach the gospel he did. They implied that Paul was some sort of demagogue, merely trying to win public favor. The first part of Paul's letter is intended to kick the legs out from under the attacks of the false teachers. It is Paul's personal defense. Why did he defend himself so vigorously? Paul defended his apostolic authority in order to defend his message. The glory of God was at stake and so was the eternal destiny of the Galatians.

1. Recall a time when you were falsely accused. Did your accuser resort to personal attacks rather than focusing on the issue? Describe how you felt.

Read Galatians 1:1-10.

2. In verses 1-5, what does Paul say about God? About Christ? About himself?

3. What does the phrase "rescue us" in verse 4 teach us about the nature of salvation?

4. What other facts about salvation do you find in verses 1-5?

♦ **5.** What is the most serious consequence of accepting a different gospel (verse 6)?

♦ *Indicates further information in Leader's Notes*

♦ **6.** How does Paul react toward those who were perverting the gospel of Christ (verses 8-9)?

Note: "The false teachers were evidently Judaizers, whose 'gospel' is summarized in Acts 15:1. They did not deny that you must believe in Jesus for salvation, but they stressed that you must be circumcised and keep the law as well. In other words, you must let Moses finish what Christ has begun. Or rather, you yourself must finish, by your obedience to the law, what Christ has begun. You must add your works to the work of Christ" (John R.W. Stott, *Only One Way, The Bible Speaks Today Series*, p. 22. Downers Grove, Ill.: InterVarsity Press, 1968).

7. What was Paul's attitude about pleasing people (verse 10)?

8. Finish this statement according to your own understanding, "The true gospel is . . ."

9. Paul ends his first paragraph with a doxology (verse 5). Take time now to thank God for his salvation and for the people he has used to communicate the gospel to you.

CALLED BY GOD

Galatians 1:11-24

As Paul continues his personal defense, he makes it clear that the gospel he preached was not his invention—it was a direct revelation from God. He underscores this by his personal history. Before his conversion, Paul was a violent persecutor of the church, determined to stamp it out. In that frame of mind, only God could change him—and God did!

1. Tell about someone you know who was once hostile to Christ but is now his follower. What brought about the change?

Read Galatians 1:11-24.

2. How did Paul learn the gospel he preached (verse 12)? What accusation would this answer?

3. Skim Acts 9:1-31 for more details about Paul's conversion story. What were some characteristics of Paul's former life? What was his original goal in life? What had motivated him?

4. What new life goal did Paul adopt (verse 16)? What caused the switch (verses 15-16)?

♦ 5. Trace on the map (page 5) the places Paul went after he met Jesus Christ. Where possible, note the time period he spent in each place.

◆ **6.** Why do you think Paul went to Arabia (verse 17)?

7. Why did the Christians of Judea praise God because of Paul (verse 24)? What might this tell us about the way we should view people who are still fighting against Christ?

8. In what ways is your personal experience an important part of your witness to others? In what ways does your life demonstrate the reality of the gospel?

9. Briefly state your own goal in life. How has knowing Jesus affected your life goal? How else should it?

TRUTH IN DANGER

Galatians 2:1-10

Although Paul was hotly defending issues that went to the very heart of the gospel, he never lost his balanced perspective—he knew when to be dogmatic and when to be flexible. Paul refused to submit to the bondage of legalism that "false brothers" were propagating, because the truth of the gospel was at stake. But Paul also needed the support of those who had found Christ before him because the false teachers were insinuating that he preached a different gospel from the other apostles. He had a healthy fear of "running in vain," so he discussed his ideas with other Christian leaders. These leaders recognized the grace God had given to Paul. They accepted him and affirmed him in his ministry to the Gentiles.

1. In what ways might the gospel be endangered today? If you have ever been asked to defend the gospel, tell about your experience.

Read Galatians 2:1-10.

    2. Why did Paul go to Jerusalem (verse 2)?

♦   **3.** Of what significance was it that he brought Titus (verse 3)?

    4. What form of opposition did Paul encounter during his visit (verse 4)?

    5. Why might the "false brothers" have been afraid to let the gospel spread to the Gentiles?

♦ **6.** What was Paul's response to the opposition (verse 5)? What reason does he give for his response?

♦ **7.** What were the results of the Jerusalem visit (verses 3-9)?

8. What advice did the apostles give to Paul (verse 10)? How does caring for the poor relate to preaching the gospel?

9. In your discussion about Christianity with others, on what issues do you take an attitude similar to Paul's in verse 5? When is compromise appropriate?

Note: Martin Luther said, "Now, as concerning faith we ought to be invincible, and more hard, if it might be, than the adamant stone; but as touching charity, we ought to be soft, and more flexible than the reed or leaf that is

shaken with the wind, and ready to yield to everything"
(James Clarke, *Commentary on the Epistle to the Galatians,* p. 112, 1953).

10. Pray about one area where you need to become more dogmatic and one area where you need to be more flexible.

PAUL CONFRONTS PETER

Galatians 2:11-21

Paul was not the only strong personality in the infant church. Peter, too, had made his presence felt. But the same fear of people that had once caused Peter to deny Christ had led him to retreat to the safety of segregation, denying the unity of Jew and Gentile—the very unity Christ died to win. Paul could not ignore this difference of opinion. To do so would not be diplomatic tact, but a denial of the truth of the gospel. Paul had lived under the allegiance to the law that Peter was defending—and it led him to zealous persecution of the Christians. The driving force in his new life was not a law, but a person. He was now free to live with complete confidence in Christ.

1. When was the first time you remember encountering prejudice? How did it affect you?

Read Galatians 2:11-21.

♦ **2.** Why did Paul confront Peter in public (verses 11-14)?

♦ **3.** Why was Peter's cowardly behavior especially odd (see Acts 10–11:18)?

4. How was Peter using his influence on others (verse 13)?

5. What groups or ideas within the church today pressure us to alter the gospel? How and when does God want you to confront these groups or ideas?

6. In Paul's day, how were people attempting to be "justified by observing the law" (verse 16)?

7. In what ways are people caught up with the same struggle today?

8. What difference would it make to you if Paul's gospel was wrong and you did have to earn your way to God by keeping the Jewish law?

♦ **9.** In verse 21, what logical conclusion does Paul point out to his rule-keeping opponents?

10. To what extent is verse 20 true of you? What is the evidence? What actions and attitudes in your life need to be subjected to the lordship of Christ?

CONTINUE AS YOU BEGAN

Galatians 3:1-14

The false teachers in Galatia were waging a theological attack on Christianity. They claimed that to be fully Christian, a person must believe in Jesus *and* become a good Jew, by being circumcised and following the Law.

Because of his background as a Pharisee, Paul fully understood the mind of the Judaizers and why they clung so doggedly to Judaism. So Paul said to these false teachers, "OK, I understand why you still think Judaism is superior to faith in Jesus Christ, but I'm going to show you from your own Scriptures why you are wrong." Here Paul moves from a personal defense to a theological defense.

1. Why do you think people want to work for salvation?

Read Galatians 3:1-14.

2. What was it about the Galatian Christians that exasperated Paul (verses 1-5)?

3. What does Paul point out about the nature of their conversion to Christ? What are the implications of this for continuing a life with Christ?

♦ **4.** Why do you think it was so clever and important for Paul to link Abraham with the principle of faith (verses 6-9)?

♦ **5.** The "legalists" relied on their descent from Abraham as well as their keeping of the law for acceptance by God. What does Paul point out about who the real descendants of Abraham are?

6. Are there ways you are tempted to rely more on "human effort" (verse 3) than on faith as your approach to God? If so, how? When and in what sense is human effort good and proper?

♦ **7.** What is Paul's main point about the law (verses 10-14)?

8. What are some ways the word *redeemed* is used in everyday life today? What insight does that give you into Paul's use of the word (verses 13-14)? How does it explain your salvation?

9. What is your responsibility to people who say to you, "It doesn't really matter what religion you have; what God cares about is whether you live a good life or not"?

10. What causes you to continue putting your faith in Jesus? What makes this faith real to you?

11. Pray for someone you know who works hard to live a good life but who still needs to accept Jesus Christ as Savior.

THEN WHY WAS THE LAW GIVEN?

Galatians 3:15-29

It almost seems that Paul is waging a duel. His weapon is faith, while the Judaizers wield the Law. As the action progresses, Paul answers an important question: If the law can't save, what is its purpose? Why was it given? Paul shows that the law reveals sin for what it is. Like the double yellow line down the center of the highway, it makes error obvious. But it can't correct or deliver us from wrong.

1. Have you ever tried to abide by a strict set of rules (for a school, a diet, a club)? What was your experience?

Read Galatians 3:15-29.

    2. What truth about God does the example in verse 15 express?

◆ **3.** Explain the distinction Paul makes between "seed" and "seeds" (verse 16). Why is it important that we belong to Christ (verse 29)?

◆ **4.** What effect did the law have on God's agreement with Abraham (verse 17)?

5. What was the purpose of the law, and how did it fulfill its purpose (verses 19, 23-24)?

Note: Verse 24 describes the law as "in charge" of us or as our "schoolmaster." The idea is hard to translate from the Greek because it doesn't exist in our culture. Literally, the law was our paidagogos, *which means "child-leader." The* paidagogos *was a slave with the job of making sure the children got safely to school. The idea is that the law does not save us; it only leads us to Christ.*

6. What are the benefits of being united with Christ (verses 26-29)?

7. What does this passage say to the person who claims, "I just keep the Ten Commandments and live by the Golden Rule"?

8. In what sense are we "all one in Christ Jesus" (verse 28)? In what specific ways should this truth affect your thinking? Your words? Your actions?

FULL RIGHTS

Galatians 4:1-11

A few years ago, *Newsweek* reported the story of "millionaires on welfare." Three children were awarded huge settlements for pollution-caused illness. Each was awarded over a million dollars. But the money won't start coming to them until they're 18 years old. Meanwhile, they're living on a small monthly welfare check.

As children of God, the Galatians were "millionaires." But they weren't claiming their inheritance. Instead, they chose to live like children who had no right to the riches.

1. When have you experienced the privileges of family ties? Or, when have you felt excluded because you didn't have the rights of sonship?

Read Galatians 4:1-11.

♦ **2.** In what sense were the Galatian Christians like children (verses 1-7)?

♦ **3.** In what sense were they like slaves?

4. Verses 4-7 contain the story of salvation. Organize the facts as if for a newspaper story: What happened? Who was responsible? When did it happen? Why did it happen? What would you give as a headline for the story?

5. What are the implications for your life of being a child of God and his heir (verses 6-7)?

Note: Abba is an Aramaic word (the language Jesus spoke). It is a close personal word for "Father," like "Daddy" or "Papa." Jesus called his Father Abba when he was praying desperately in the garden before his arrest (Mark 14:36).

◆ **6.** Earthly parents seek to bring their children to the point of maturity and independence. How is our sonship with God similar to and different from our relationship with our earthly parents?

7. What problem did Paul point to in verses 8-11? What did this reveal about his readers?

8. In what ways are you tempted to think or act as you did before you became a Christian? What precautions could you take now to squash these temptations before they come?

9. Ask your heavenly Father to help you understand how being a son or daughter of God should alter your actions today.

PAUL'S CONCERN

Galatians 4:12-31

Paul has been outlining a careful argument, based on Scripture and theological thought. Now, right in the middle of this argument, Paul appeals to the Galatians with deep personal feeling. This is no detached, scholarly approach. Here Paul speaks with a warm, fatherly tone, recalling past experiences and warm personal relationships. He also gives us fascinating glimpses into his ministry and physical needs, leaving us with a curiosity to know more about this man who says, "Become like me."

1. Who is your hero—the person you would most like to imitate in your life?

Read Galatians 4:12-20.

2. In what sense would Paul want his readers to become like himself (verse 12)?

♦ **3.** How had he become like them? What ministry principles can we draw from Paul's example?

4. What clues do you pick up about the apostle's condition (verses 12-15)? (See also 2 Corinthians 12:7-10 and Galatians 6:11.)

5. How had the Galatians responded to Paul's physical need?

6. What caused the change in the Galatians' response to Paul (verses 16-17)?

7. What are some of the words and metaphors Paul uses to express his emotions toward the Galatians?

8. What is Paul's ultimate concern for the Galatian Christians (verse 19)?

9. Looking back over the last year, what evidence can you identify that indicates Christ is being formed in you?

Read Galatians 4:21-31.

    10. Who is Paul challenging in these verses? Where does Paul get "ammunition" for his counterattack? (See verse 21.)

    11. If your time permits, read the background of Paul's reference to Sarah and Hagar in Genesis 16–17, and 21:1-21. Summarize by jotting down the significant details of that story here.

♦ **12.** What point is Paul making by unfolding this portion of Jewish history (verses 24-31)?

    13. Pray that you will be so satisfied with the salvation Jesus has given you that you, like Paul, will be able to say, "Become like me."

FREE FOR A PURPOSE

Galatians 5

Leaving home is an essential step toward growth. But the process can be painful! On the one hand, a son or daughter may use this new freedom to overindulge in things that were once forbidden. On the other hand, parents can refuse to let go, insisting on control.

The Galatians were free from the bondage of keeping the Jewish law in order to receive salvation. But, like parents who are unable to let go of a child, some of the Galatians were trying to reimpose the Jewish law on Christians. Others were abusing their new freedom in Christ. "If Christ has set us free," they reasoned, "we can do as we please."

Paul addresses both of these extremes. He says we will know we have truly understood Christian freedom when we see the fruits of the Spirit in our lives. And we'll practice these things not because we have to, but because we want to. That's the secret of freedom in Christ.

1. What "spiritual yardstick" does your church circle use in deciding who "measures up"?

Read Galatians 5:1-12.

2. From what had Christ set the Galatians free? What, then, is the significance of Paul's terse command "stand firm"?

3. In Paul's opinion, what would agreeing to be circumcised indicate about the Galatians (verses 3-4)?

4. In what ways do twentieth-century Christians give in to legalism? What outward things do we substitute for a true and living walk with God?

5. What is most important in the Christian life, according to Paul (verse 6)?

◆ **6.** How does Paul view the actions and teaching of those who were trying to influence the Galatians (verses 7-12)?

Read Galatians 5:13-26.

◆ **7.** According to Paul, how are we to guard against abusing our freedom in Christ (verses 13-15)? Give one example of how you've seen this safeguard working in your life.

8. What dichotomy does Paul point out in verses 16-17? Do you agree with him? Why or why not?

9. Which of the Spirit products in verses 22-23 show up most often in your life? Which ones are lacking?

10. What will you do this week to "keep in step with the Spirit" (verse 25)?

ALL THAT COUNTS

Galatians 6

The fruit of the Spirit (Galatians 5:22-23) is immediately put into practice in Paul's closing words. The legalists impose burdens; Christians bear them for others.

The cross of Christ is the center of Paul's gospel. It was the controlling principle of his life. "May I never boast except in the cross of our Lord Jesus Christ" (6:14). Paul's final challenge and benediction grow out of this perspective.

1. What is one thing you'd love to boast about if you had the chance?

Read Galatians 6:1-10.

2. How should we react when fellow Christians sin (verses 1-2)? By implication, how should we *not* react?

♦ **3.** How do you reconcile verses 2 and 5? In what sense do we have responsibilities no one else can share?

4. In what creative ways, in addition to financial giving, could you share good things with those who are helping you to mature spiritually (verse 6)?

♦ **5.** What is the difference between sowing to please the sinful nature and sowing to please the Spirit (verses 7-8)? How can you avoid legalism in making this distinction?

6. What does Paul mean by the phrase "doing good" (verses 9-10)? What opportunities do you have right now to put this into practice? To whom do Christians have a special responsibility?

Read Galatians 6:11-18.

7. What rewards were the Judaizers really after (verse 12)? What did they hope to avoid?

8. What perspective had the cross given to Paul's priorities in life?

9. Verse 15 expresses Paul's chief concern in writing this letter. If he were writing today, what things might he put in the place of circumcision and uncircumcision?

10. Sing together Isaac Watts' hymn, based on verse 14:

When I survey the wondrous cross
On which the Prince of glory died,
My richest gain I count but loss,
And pour contempt on all my pride.

Forbid it, Lord, that I should boast
Save in the death of Christ my God;
All the vain things that charm me most,
I sacrifice them to His blood.

INTRODUCTION TO TITUS

Titus is a New Testament figure who is often overlooked when we think of key people in the growth of the early church. Yet Titus was Paul's close companion and was involved in some of the most significant events that took place in the years after Jesus' death.

As we saw in Galatians, Titus helped Paul to defuse one of the early church's most explosive problems: could Gentiles receive salvation without first subjecting themselves to Mosaic Law? Paul brought Titus to Jerusalem as an example of an uncircumcised believer. Fortunately for the church, Paul and Titus made their point. Later, Titus was a central figure in smoothing over the difficulties that had developed in the church at Corinth.

By the time Paul began to write the letter you are about to study, Titus had been given a new assignment: oversight of the believers on the island of Crete. Although Paul had apparently started the church at Crete, Titus's task was to maintain it and ensure its continued growth.

Here Paul instructs Titus about issues such as leadership in the church, rooting out false teachers, and relationships within the church. The instructions he offers to Titus are as helpful today as they were in Paul's day. The letter ends with a summary of basic principles for Christian living—a theme that in one form or another can be found in almost every one of Paul's letters.

THE MARKS OF A GOOD LEADER

Titus 1

Paul was concerned about the well-being of the churches he established. Evidently there was a need for more definite organization and stronger leadership in the churches of Crete, an island with a negative reputation. In many ways, our modern Western society is like that of ancient Crete—built around pleasure, excess, and selfishness. We can learn a great deal from Paul's instructions about living as a Christian in such an environment.

1. How would you identify the greatest challenge your church is facing now?

Read Titus 1:1-16.

2. In verses 1-4, what can you learn about God? About Paul? About Titus?

3. What details about Titus's assignment do you find here (verse 5)?

♦ **4.** What problems does he face in accomplishing the task Paul has given him (verses 10-14)?

5. What observations can you make about the qualifications for leaders in verses 6-9? What impresses you most about these qualities?

6. Think about a leader who has had a strong, positive influence on your life. Which of these qualities made that person effective?

7. If your church were looking for qualified leaders according to this passage, how would you measure up?

8. In what context does Paul use the phrase, "to the pure, all things are pure" (verse 15)? What does the phrase mean for you today?

9. What does verse 16 teach you about salvation? How do your actions show that you know God?

10. Which qualities in verses 8-9 do you most desire to develop in your life? What steps can you take toward this goal this week?

WHAT TO TEACH (AND WHO TO TEACH)

Titus 2 and 3

Paul never separates doctrine from behavior. Correct doctrine and godly behavior are bound together in this passage. Paul instructs Titus to teach doctrine and obedient action to all the different groups in the church. There is a challenge here for everyone.

1. Tell about an older man or woman who has been influential in your life.

Read Titus 2:1–3:2.

2. Choose one word that describes Paul's message to each of the following groups: older men (2:2); older women (2:3); younger women (2:4-5); younger men (2:6-8); slaves (2:9-10).

◆ **3.** For what reasons did Paul want the various groups to obey his teaching (2:5, 10)?

4. Why do you think Paul emphasizes self control (2:2, 5-6, 12) and doing "what is good" (2:3, 7, 14; 3:1)?

5. In order to live self-controlled lives, Paul instructs his readers to say no to certain things. What are they? What things do you need to say no to in your life?

6. What direct effects does Christ's coming return have on your actions (2:13-14)? How else should it affect you?

7. A Greek historian noted that the Cretans were regularly involved in "insurrection, murder, and internecine wars." What light does this shed on Paul's reminder in 3:1-2?

Read Titus 3:3-15.

8. How does Paul describe life before Christ? What were you like before God's mercy touched your life? How did you change?

9. From verses 4-7, what can you learn about God's character and work in us?

10. What does Paul stress again about the response of those who trust in God (verses 8, 14)?

11. How does Paul say a divisive person should be treated (verse 10)?

♦ **12.** How do Paul's final remarks reinforce his theme of "doing good" (verses 12-15)?

13. How can you "do good" in a way that will have a significant impact on those you interact with daily?

INTRODUCTION TO PHILEMON

Philemon is Paul's shortest and most personal letter. The situation he addresses is quite simple. Onesimus, Philemon's slave, had run away, and in the process he met Paul and became a believer in Jesus. The apostle then sent Onesimus back to his owner, who was also a Christian, with this letter, asking the owner to accept the slave back as a brother in Christ.

Paul's other letters show him to be a brilliant theologian. This letter, however, reveals an apostle who would use any approach he could think of to convince God's people to accept one another. It is a fascinating and practical view of love in action.

RADICAL FORGIVENESS

Philemon

This letter must be read against the dark background of slavery in the Roman Empire, where slaves (over half the population) had no rights and where they were subject to the most extreme punishment at the whim of their masters.

This letter of intercession is one of the world's masterpieces of personal correspondence. Notice Paul's tact as he begins, not by affirming his apostolic authority, but by referring to himself as "a prisoner of Christ Jesus." He sends affectionate greetings, pays Philemon a deserved compliment, and then makes his appeal for the runaway slave. In this letter Paul sets the highest example of Christian courtesy and consideration.

1. When have you needed to forgive someone who wronged you? What emotions did you experience?

Read Philemon 1-25.

2. What benefit of sharing one's faith does Paul point out (verse 6)? In what ways has this been your experience?

♦ **3.** Describe Paul's feelings for Onesimus (verses 8-14). How might these feelings have affected Philemon?

♦ **4.** Why was Onesimus formerly useless to Philemon (verses 11, 18)? How and why had he become useful to him (verse 16)?

5. What good does Paul see in Onesimus's running away from Philemon (verses 15-16)?

6. What things does Paul add to the end of the letter to ensure that Philemon accepts Onesimus back (verses 17-22)?

♦ **7.** Do you think this letter is a sincere request or an example of crafty persuasive technique? Why?

♦ **8.** In what ways can the story of Paul and Onesimus be seen as a parable of our own redemption?

9. Which of the qualities in verses 4-7 need to become more a part of your daily experience? How can your study group encourage you in this desire?

10. Think about a relationship you know of that needs healing. How might you serve as a "Paul" in helping to bring about reconciliation?

LEADER'S NOTES

◼ Study 1/Sent by God

Question 5. Galatians 1:6 makes it clear that it is not Paul the Galatians are deserting; it is God himself. By turning away from the gospel of grace, they are also turning away from the God of grace.

Question 6. Paul's judgment against the Judaizers may seem strong, but we need to remember what was at stake. As Barclay says, "It is a strange thing to think that, if Paul's opponents had had their way, the gospel might have been kept for Jews, and we might never have had the chance to know the love of Christ" (William Barclay, *The Letters to the Galatians and Ephesians,* p. 1. Saint Andrew Press, 1966).

◼ Study 2/Called by God

Question 5. Paul's travels included: Arabia (Galatians 1:17); Damascus (1:17); Jerusalem (1:18) (he arrived after three years and stayed two weeks); Syria and Cilicia (1:21); and Jerusalem (2:1) (he returned fourteen years later).

Question 6. This is the only place Paul mentions his "retreat" into Arabia. Perhaps he went away into a desert area, taking the Scriptures with him to re-study the Messiah. He seems to have stayed there three years (Galatians 1:18).

■ **Study 3/Truth in Danger**

Question 3. The Judaizers claimed that only the Jews had privileges with God, so that before a man could become a Christian, he had to become a Jew by being circumcised. Titus was a test case. As a Greek, would they force him to become a Jew before he could be a Christian?

Question 6. Paul stood firm as a rock against this heresy. To yield would have been to accept the slavery of the law and to deny freedom in Christ.

Question 7. Paul's determination won the day. Paul was affirmed in his call to work among the Gentiles while the others would continue to minister among the Jews. Both would preach the same gospel— freedom in Christ.

■ **Study 4/Paul Confronts Peter**

Question 2. In the last study (Galatians 2:1-10), Paul and Peter had been at one in their teaching. Even now, it was not Peter's teaching that Paul was condemning, but his behavior. Peter was preaching one thing (unity and freedom in Christ) and practicing another (withdrawing from Gentile believers). This was no trivial matter— the truth of the gospel was at stake. Paul could not tolerate deviation from this truth, especially from a leader like Peter.

Question 3. Peter had been given a direct, special revelation from God on this very subject only a short time previous to this encounter.

He could not have forgotten this. But now he lacked the courage of his conviction and was giving in to a pressure group. The same Peter who denied his Lord for fear of a maidservant was now denying the gospel for fear of the Judaizers.

Question 9. Paul points out that if salvation is our own work, then Christ's work was unnecessary. John Stott says, "There are large numbers of people who, like the Judaizers, are making these very mistakes. They are seeking to commend themselves to God by their own works. They think it noble to try to win their way to God and to heaven. But it is not noble; it is dreadfully ignoble. For, in effect, it is to deny both the nature of God and the mission of Christ. It is to refuse to let God be gracious. It is to tell Christ that He need not have bothered to die. For both the grace of God and the death of Christ become redundant if we are masters of our own destiny and can save ourselves" (John R.W. Stott, *Only One Way, The Bible Speaks Today Series,* p. 22. Downers Grove, Ill.: InterVarsity Press, 1968).

◼ Study 5/Continue As You Began

Question 4. "To a Jew the authority of Abraham was decisive. Paul shows that theologically, Abraham was accepted by God through faith, not works. Scripture thus corroborates Paul's gospel and their own experience" (Samuel J. Mikolaski, *The New Bible Commentary: Revised, Galatians,* p. 1097. Grand Rapids, Mich.: Eerdmans, 1970).

Question 5. Abraham was the father of the Jews. The Judaizers were teaching that the Galatians should become true children of Abraham through circumcision. Paul says that the Galatian Christians are already children of Abraham—not through circumcision, but through faith.

Question 7. Since everyone has failed to keep the law (except Jesus), Paul concludes that "All who rely on observing the law are under a curse" (Galatians 3:10). The law does not justify—it condemns. Trying to be justified by keeping the law leads to a dead end.

■ Study 6/Then Why Was the Law Given?

Question 3. God promised an inheritance to Abraham and his ancestors. While the immediate and literal object of this promise was the land of Canaan, Paul knew that this was not the ultimate fulfillment of the promise. "God said that in Abraham's seed all the families of the earth would be blessed, and how could the whole world be blessed through Jews living in the land of Canaan? Paul realized that both the 'land' which was promised and the 'seed' to whom it was promised were ultimately spiritual. God's purpose was not just to give the land of Canaan to the Jews, but to give salvation (a spiritual inheritance) to believers who are in Christ" *(Only One Way,* p. 88). The singular use of the word *seed* refers to Christ and to all those who are in Christ by faith.

Question 4. The promise to Abraham was a free gift. The Judaizers claimed that the Christian inheritance is given to those who keep the law. Paul affirms in Galatians 3:18 that the inheritance depends on God's promise, not on keeping the law.

■ Study 7/Full Rights

Question 2. "For Paul, the man who governed his life by slavery to the law was still a child; the man who had learned the way of grace had become a mature, full-grown man in the Christian faith" *(The Letters to the Galatians and Ephesians,* p. 38).

Question 3. Though the Galatians had technically never been under the law, their turning to legalism was turning to an old system God had discontinued; therefore, it meant regressing to slavery.

Question 6. Freedom does not mean independence. The mature Christian still recognizes the need and privilege of calling God *Abba* or "Father." As Christians, we have not "come of age" in the sense that we can live outside the scope of God's fatherly care. In fact, as we mature, we become more and more dependent on him.

■ Study 8/Paul's Concern

Question 3. "In seeking to win other people for Christ, our end is to make them like us, while the means to that end is to make ourselves like them. If they are to become one with us in Christian conviction and experience, we must first become one with them in Christian compassion. We must be able to say with the apostle Paul: 'I became like you; now you become like me'" *(Only One Way,* p. 113).

Question 12. The legalists, who insisted on ceremonial observance of the law as a means to salvation, are likened to Hagar's offspring. They are the children of a slave and will always be in bondage to the law. Paul contrasts these "children of slavery" with the "children of promise." Children of promise, like Isaac, are not born in any ordinary way. They are born by the power of the Spirit.

■ Study 9/Free for a Purpose

Question 6. Paul uses the metaphor of yeast and dough to show that "a small portion of legalism, if it be mixed with the gospel, corrupts its purity. To add legal ordinances and works in the least degree to justification by faith is to undermine the whole" (Robert Jamieson,

A.R. Fausset, and David Brown, *Commentary on the Whole Bible,* p. 1274. Grand Rapids, Mich.: Zondervan, 1961).

Question 7. Freedom means love, not license. A total absence of limits is a perversion of what freedom really is. As G. Campbell Morgan wrote, "A room is not a room that has no walls; so liberty is not liberty that has no boundaries."

■ Study 10/All That Counts

Question 3. We need to help other Christians, and they need to help us. But we shouldn't sit back and depend on somebody else to live our lives for us, blaming them if we fail. We're responsible for our own actions. On the day of judgment, each of us will be accountable to God individually.

Question 5. "If a man is faithful and conscientious in his sowing, then he can confidently expect a good harvest. If he 'sows wild oats,' as we sometimes say, then he must not expect to reap strawberries!" *(Only One Way,* p. 166).

■ Study 11/The Marks of a Good Leader

Question 4. Titus 1:10 refers to "the circumcision group." These were the Jewish legalists Paul argued against in the book of Galatians. "Legalism is the universal and persistent enemy of grace" (Paul F. Barackman, *Proclaiming the New Testament, The Epistles to Timothy and Titus,* p. 140. Grand Rapids, Mich.: Baker, 1962).

■ Study 12/What to Teach (and Who to Teach)

Question 3. Paul speaks of making "the teaching about God our Savior attractive" (Titus 2:10). In the Greek, the idea is that of arranging jewels to set off their full beauty.

Question 12. With this emphasis on "doing what is good," Paul ends one of the last letters he wrote. It is quite possible that he was arrested soon after this and sent to Rome for his final trial and execution.

■ Study 13/Radical Forgiveness

Question 3. Paul is so sympathetic to the plight of Onesimus that he is willing to deprive himself of Onesimus's help as well as to pay Philemon for any loss Onesimus has caused him. With his own hand he wrote what was legally a promissory note, obligating himself to pay the debt Onesimus owed.

Question 4. Notice that in Philemon 11 Paul makes a gentle pun on Onesimus's name, which means "useful."

Question 7. Paul's willingness to place himself under financial obligation for Onesimus demonstrates his sincerity.

Question 8. Martin Luther said, "We are all God's Onesimi, to my thinking." We are all sinners by nature, and indeed, we were slaves to sin. But Christ died to make us free (see Galatians 5:1).

WHAT SHOULD WE STUDY NEXT?

To help your group answer that question, we've listed the Fisherman Guides by category so you can choose your next study.

TOPICAL STUDIES

Angels, Wright

Becoming Women of Purpose, Barton

Building Your House on the Lord, Brestin

Discipleship, Reapsome

Doing Justice, Showing Mercy, Wright

Encouraging Others, Johnson

Examining the Claims of Jesus, Brestin

Friendship, Brestin

The Fruit of the Spirit, Briscoe

Great Doctrines of the Bible, Board

Great Passages of the Bible, Plueddemann

Great Prayers of the Bible, Plueddemann

Growing Through Life's Challenges, Reapsome

Guidance & God's Will, Stark

Heart Renewal, Goring

Higher Ground, Brestin

Lifestyle Priorities, White

Marriage, Stevens

Miracles, Castleman

Moneywise, Larsen

One Body, One Spirit, Larsen

The Parables of Jesus, Hunt

Prayer, Jones

The Prophets, Wright

Proverbs & Parables, Brestin

Satisfying Work, Stevens & Schoberg

Senior Saints, Reapsome

Sermon on the Mount, Hunt

Spiritual Warfare, Moreau

The Ten Commandments, Briscoe

Who Is God? Seemuth

Who Is the Holy Spirit? Knuckles & Van Reken

Who Is Jesus? Van Reken

Witnesses to All the World, Plueddemann

Worship, Sibley

BIBLE BOOK STUDIES

Genesis, Fromer & Keyes

Job, Klug

Psalms, Klug

Proverbs: Wisdom That Works, Wright

Ecclesiastes, Brestin

Jonah, Habakkuk, & Malachi, Fromer & Keyes

Matthew, Sibley

Mark, Christensen

Luke, Keyes

John: Living Word, Kuniholm

Acts 1-12, Christensen

Paul (Acts 13-28), Christensen

Romans: The Christian Story, Reapsome

1 Corinthians, Hummel

Strengthened to Serve (2 Corinthians), Plueddemann

Galatians, Titus & Philemon, Kuniholm

Ephesians, Baylis

Philippians, Klug

Colossians, Shaw

Letters to the Thessalonians, Fromer & Keyes

Letters to Timothy, Fromer & Keyes

Hebrews, Hunt

James, Christensen

1 & 2 Peter, Jude, Brestin

How Should a Christian Live? (1, 2 & 3 John), Brestin

Revelation, Hunt

BIBLE CHARACTER STUDIES

David: Man after God's Own Heart, Castleman

Elijah, Castleman

Great People of the Bible, Plueddemann

King David: Trusting God for a Lifetime, Castleman

Men Like Us, Heidebrecht & Scheuermann

Paul (Acts 13-28), Christensen

Peter, Castleman

Ruth & Daniel, Stokes

Women Like Us, Barton

Women Who Achieved for God, Christensen

Women Who Believed God, Christensen